Sick & Tired Series

Why Doesn't God Fix It?

Shining Eternal Light on the

Darkness of Chronic Illness

and Any Suffering

KIMBERLY RAE

Why Doesn't God Fix It? by Kimberly Rae takes on the big question everybody asks sooner or later: If God is so loving, why does He let bad things happen? Right up front, Rae clarifies that she does not have a definitive answer, but she does have biblical support for what she believes to be the case. Saddled with multiple chronic health issues....Instead of wallowing in self-pity, as so many choose to do, Rae turned to the Bible for answers to her own personal questions. In *Why Doesn't God Fix It?* she does a superb job of calling upon the examples Jesus gave us when he walked the Earth as a human being. As one who has also been saddled with a number of chronic health issues due to no fault of my own (i.e. nothing I did "caused" my lupus, hearing loss, or vision deficiencies), I was personally pleased to find the author and I were already of one mind.

Why Doesn't God Fix It? is a very professionally written biblical response to the titular question. As someone who often ignores appendices when I read a book, I felt obliged to read Rae's appendices in order to provide an accurate review. I am glad I did, because those appendices were filled with information as valuable as the body of the book. In fact, for one appendix she realized and admitted she had avoided a couple uncomfortable Bible verses that were easier to ignore than to rectify, so she dove in head first and tackled those verses quite astutely. All in all, *Why Doesn't God Fix It?* is well written, easily readable, biblically correct and logically defensible....This is a book that should be in every church's library. It would also make a very good text for a special Sunday School class or small-group read, particularly for any members suffering from a "why me?" response to their health concerns.

5-Star Review by Lee Ashford for Readers' Favorite

For more information on this book and the author visit
www.kimberlyrae.com

Library of Congress Control Number: 2015913849
Library of Congress Cataloging-in-Publication Data
Rae, Kimberly.
Why Doesn't God Fix It?/ Kimberly Rae
Sick & Tired Series Book Three
1st Edition, November 2014
2nd Edition, September 2015
3rd Edition, August 2021

Printed in the United States of America.
ISBN-13: 978-1502309181
ISBN-10: 1502309181

Why Doesn't God Fix It?

Sick & Tired Series

SICK & TIRED
But You Don't Look Sick!
It's Not Fair—Giving Yourself Permission to Grieve
Losing Your Identity to Sickness
How to Explain Your Illness so People Don't Think You're Faking It

YOU'RE SICK, THEY'RE NOT
Chronic Illness Changes Relationships
Why Did God Do This to My Family?
Illness and Your Love Language
Chronic Illness and Your Personality Type

YOU'RE SICK, THEY'RE NOT BIBLE STUDY COMPANION

WHY DOESN'T GOD FIX IT?
Bribing God
The What Ifs and If Onlys
Illness and Depression
God I'll Trust You If…

WHY DOESN'T GOD FIX IT? BIBLE STUDY COMPANION

LAUGHTER FOR THE SICK & TIRED
Funny Stories and Jokes, Just for Fun

HELP FOR THE SICK & TIRED
Fun medical "cures" from the past.
All the Advice you Never Wanted
To Church or Not to Church
I Believe You

Available in paperback and e-book.

DEDICATION

*To my little sister, Rachel, for all the times
through thyroid cancer and everything else when
I'm sure you've wanted to ask why and haven't
gotten an answer.*

*I love you more
than calcium chews!*

Table of Contents:

Introduction—Why Does God Let Bad Things Happen?

Chapter 1 Bribing God.. 7

Chapter 2 The Feelings of Our Infirmities.............................19

Chapter 3 Not Enough Faith?.....................................31

Chapter 4 Why Didn't Jesus Heal Everybody?......................41

Chapter 5 The Annoying Voice Inside My Head...................51

Chapter 6 God I'll Trust You If................................63

Chapter 7 Illness and Depression...............................75

Chapter 8 The If Onlys and What Ifs.......................89

Chapter 9 Hurting Alone...103

Chapter 10 When the Mountain won't Move.....................115

Conclusion—Fearfully and Wonderfully Made

Appendix A: Who is this God?

Appendix B: Jesus, Healing, and Faith
A walk through the book of Matthew, searching for answers
from Jesus by one who has not been healed.

Appendix C: The Bible Vs. Health & Wealth
A study through the book of Matthew seeking God's perspective
on health and wealth.

INTRODUCTION

WHY DOES GOD LET
BAD THINGS HAPPEN?

The question is as old as humanity. The Book of Job, considered by many the oldest of the Scriptures, is centered on it. And in an eternal twist of irony, though over thirty chapters are devoted to Job's friends' faulty answers, Job's own faulty answers, and even a large speech by God Himself, the real answer is never actually revealed.

Do I presume to give the answer to the book's title, *Why Doesn't God Fix It?* No. This book will not give an answer that will satisfy a question people have been asking for millennia.

So should you stop reading now and toss this in the trash? I hope not. For one, you would have wasted your money and that's not very practical. For another, just talking about the nature of the question itself has benefit, in my opinion (obviously, or I wouldn't be writing this now).

The biggest reason I believe you should take the time to read this book is because I am convinced that, though the full answer is unattainable in this life, I think we can find a glimpse of it, enough of a glimpse that we can live in hope despite the blanks in the answer that will not be filled before eternity.

I invite you to come with me. Let's ask the right questions, and search together for that glimpse of an answer. Though faint and sometimes flickering, that small glimpse has such light behind it that I believe we can anchor our hope upon it and live with joy, even in suffering.

Sometimes God does not give the answer because He knows He is all the answer we really need. In finding Him, we find enough.

Will you walk toward Him with me? It's okay if right now the questions you want to ask Him are laced with pain, anger, or even bitterness. He can handle them. Only be willing to listen to what He has to say in response. Like Job, don't listen to the friends trying to convince you God is punishing you, and definitely don't listen to those who, like Job's wife, say you should just curse God and die. Instead, like Job, go to God Himself with your grief, your anger, your defense.

I'll go with you. You might be surprised what He has to say to us all.

The secret things belong to the Lord our God, but those things which are revealed belong to us and to our children forever.
Deuteronomy 29:29

CHAPTER ONE

BRIBING GOD

Do you use God to solve your problems?
Or do you use your problems to find God?
Dr. Larry Crabb[i]

Have you ever tried to bribe God? "God, if You get me out of this hospital, I'll go to church every Sunday for the rest of my life."

How about negotiating? "Lord, You know I could serve you a lot better if I was healthy, so…"

A half-threat? "I was thinking about going overseas on a missions trip, but I can't if I don't get better, so..."

Then there's the out-and-out threat. "If you don't take this sickness away, I'm done following You or even believing in You."

If we admit our deepest thoughts, most of us would have to say we've at least felt, if not said, some version of every one of the above. That is a frightening thought. Will God get angry? Will lightning come down to obliterate us?

Well, if you're still reading this, lightning hasn't struck you yet, so that's good. Even more encouraging, God's Book, the Bible, is full of people just like us, or maybe worse; people who whined or cried or asked why, or had grown-up temper tantrums to a God who just wasn't doing things the way they thought He should.

Here are just a few:

Job: He's convinced he's righteous and doesn't deserve the horror he's experiencing. He never curses God, but he does talk about how he wishes he'd been born dead. Many of his questions and statements are legitimate. God does not coddle him or even respond to his burning questions. Instead, God tells Job to respond to him like a man, then goes on to present His amazing power until Job recognizes that maybe he doesn't know everything, and he isn't God, so he'll shut his mouth and pray for his friends instead. (Book of Job)

Elijah: After one of the biggest spiritual victories of all time, Elijah runs off, wears himself out, and is so exhausted and worn down physically and emotionally, he asks God to kill him. God doesn't lecture Elijah or try to snap him out of his thoughts. He knows what Elijah needs: sleep and food. After eating, sleeping, eating and sleeping some more, when Elijah's body is rejuvenated enough for his mind to follow, then God gives him a dose of encouraging reality, motivating him to get back in the fight, but not until his strength is restored. (1 Kings 18-19)

David: The Psalms are full of emotional chapters which, if the poetic beauty is removed, are basically a man asking God why He doesn't fix it. Some of the most powerful psalms are when David was asking the hardest questions:

Where are you, God?

Why are you letting this happen to me?

Don't you care about me at all? Don't you see how much I've cried?

But then David ends with what he knows to be true, even though he probably doesn't feel it right then. He chooses to recognize God's goodness and justice, and places his faith back where it should be—on what he knows to be true rather than what he feels, which is probably one of the reasons God called David a man after His own heart (Acts 13:22). (Book of Psalms)

Sarah: She didn't have much to say to God, but Sarah's actions in Genesis 16 were one big declaration that God wasn't doing things her way and she was going to fix her problems herself. God had promised to give her a son, but after being barren for so many years, and the target of cultural misconceptions that it meant God had cursed her, Sarah decided to help God out. He was moving way too slow. God still did what He promised He would do, but Sarah's jumping in to fix things herself had bad ramifications that are still affecting nations today. The lesson in that? Better to let it all out in your prayers and wait for God to respond than to take matters into your own hands. (Genesis 16)

Now onto One not like us and yet who understands:

Jesus: As surprising and even impossible as it may seem, Jesus Himself had moments where He questioned God the Father. And since He and the Father are one, if He had questions, it seems pretty reasonable that we will, too! Jesus, in His moments of deepest physical and spiritual despair, asked God to take away His cup of suffering (but then ended saying God's will should be done—a good prayer to follow), and on the cross He even called out the ultimate question: Why? *"My God, my God, why have you forsaken me?"* (Mark 15:34) Being perfectly God and man, Jesus knew why. He knew He was taking on the sins of the world and it would be the one and only time in all eternity that God the Father would be separated from God the Son. He even knew the separation would not last (Hebrews 12:2), but how agonizing that moment must have been, agonizing enough to cry out in pain and ask, "Why?" (Books Matthew, Mark, Luke, John)

So, if some of God's most heroic characters had their times of angry, depressed or even bitter diatribes, what does that mean for you?

1. **You are not alone**. If you feel desperate, like you'd promise God anything if He'd just take away the pain, you're not the first to feel that way and you certainly will not be the last.

2. **God can handle your feelings.** Even if your feelings are not the kind you could say in church, you can say them to God. Strange, isn't it? Sometimes Christians get scared when we are real rather than "spiritual." If David came into many churches and read his poetry aloud, people would gasp and whisper about his scandalously un-Christian feelings. God isn't threatened by our humanity. He knows all about it, more than we do really. He knows how we struggle and why, and our transparent expression of our feelings will get the toxins out so there is room for His truth.

3. **Go ahead and tell God your feelings.** He knows them anyway. Saying them out loud is not dangerous. I know it feels that way, but the truth is that keeping them hidden and secret is actually worse. In secret, they become bigger and more powerful. If you get them out, they're out. Give your feelings to God, let the expression of them break you. You may feel saying them out loud will disintegrate the fragile hold you have on yourself, but that's okay. As long as you're going to God with them, He can hold the broken pieces of who you have become. Just don't keep them yourself. They can destroy you.

4. **Don't try to fix it yourself.** As hard as it is to trust God when things aren't happening and you're waiting for a miracle you aren't certain will ever come, jumping ahead of God and pushing forward when you know He wants you to wait only ends up badly. I've spent a lot of money, time and heartache trying things that didn't work and sometimes caused a lot of trouble, because I rushed ahead into a possibility without checking with God first.

In conclusion, if you're feeling like Job, check out who God really is. If you're feeling like Elijah, let yourself be taken care of for awhile. Stop analyzing your feelings and instead get your body the rest and nourishment it needs. If you feel like David, write or say your feelings, but then conclude them with truth. If you feel like Sarah, don't do whatever it is you're thinking of doing! Don't try to bribe, negotiate or threaten God. It doesn't work.

Most of all, like Jesus, test all things, even feelings and temptations, according to the Scriptures, and end your prayers asking that God's will be done. Hold fast to that which is true and reject what is not (1 Thess. 5:21).

No matter how dark or desperate your feelings are, take them straight to God. He's the only one strong enough to hold them, so let Him have them every time they come.

KIMBERLY RAE

Cast your burden on the Lord,
and He shall sustain you.
Psalm 55:22

Individual or Group Study Questions

1. Which of the people mentioned in this chapter do you relate to the most? Why?

2. Have you had a moment like any of those mentioned in the chapter? Describe a time when you felt like:

Job—

Elijah—

David—

Sarah—

Jesus—

3. Have you ever felt like your feelings were too bad to talk to God about?

4. Why do you think Christians sometimes fear people being transparent about their questions or negative feelings about God? Do you think there are unexplored vulnerabilities there, or people are just not wanting to deal with the really tough questions of life?

5. Have you ever tried to bribe or manipulate God? How did that go?

ACTIVITY: Tell God how you really feel. Really. Write it down if you want. Be totally honest and real, even if your feelings are as desperate as Elijah's or Job's or David's. Admit if you feel like trying to fix things on your own. Admit it if you feel like God hasn't come through for you. Let it all out, then sit and listen, and see if He has anything to say to you. Read His Word and ask Him to show you something important.

CHAPTER TWO

THE FEELINGS OF OUR INFIRMITIES

The things I cannot do are looking in through my window now and beckoning me and calling me. And His comfort, "But I am here in the room with you; I am nearer than those beckoning, calling things. I come between them and you. You have nothing to do now but to please me."
Amy Carmichael[ii]

After major surgery, weeks in ICU, seizures, fluid on the brain, multiple potentially fatal scenarios and being diagnosed with an incurable disease, I'd say I know a thing or two about infirmities. Like the fact that I have them, and I don't like them.

They come with bad stuff. Unpleasant symptoms. Long nights. Difficult emotions. False hopes. The problems are so much more than what happens within the physical body. Sometimes the worst part of infirmities is how they affect the mind and the heart.

I have learned not to trust my emotions whenever my blood sugar is unstable, or I am tapering down on my daily steroid dose after a sickness, or my asthma is flaring up and I'm not getting enough oxygen to my brain, or when I just plain feel lousy. All things considered, seems like I shouldn't be trusting my emotions very often at all!

You likely know what I mean. Your body is giving out on you, betraying you, and not only is that making life harder than you'd like it to be, but it's affecting how well you think and how you feel—about life, about relationships, about things that shouldn't be a big deal like the noise someone makes while chewing or the drip, drip, drip of a leaky faucet.

Instead, you find yourself irrational, unreasonable, and irritated at the slightest provocation, or even no provocation at all. One of the first signs for me that my asthma is flaring up (aside from not being able to breathe well of course) is that I am suddenly annoyed with everyone about everything. Like instant PMS. I'm sitting at the supper table and, out of nowhere, I have a mental sarcastic comment for every single thing that is said, even simple things like, "I like this salad." I must have a fascinating repertoire of cutting remarks stored somewhere deep in my subconscious to be able to think of something bitter to say to that!

Though I try to hold my tongue and avoid spewing my feelings on others (see *You're Sick, They're Not*, chapter "Am I Allowed to Feel Crabby Today?"), I find this aspect of sickness the hardest sometimes. We are supposed to live with self-control, not just controlling our physical actions, but bringing our thoughts into captivity as well (2 Corinthians 10:5). As Proverbs 25:28 says, *"Whoever has no rule over his own spirit is like a city broken down, without walls."* I feel like that when I'm sick, like a city left exposed and vulnerable to attack. I don't like it, but sometimes it seems like I have no control over it. I feel like I can't rule my own spirit because it is overruled by what is happening to my body.

Having my emotions so affected by my condition is frustrating. It's a never-ending battle that I feel I am sometimes waging without any weapons or armor.

However, just the other day I discovered something important, and good. Something I can cling to, even when I'm wanting to spit out angry comments at whoever said they like the salad.

I found this goodness in Hebrews 4:15, which says, *"We have not an high priest which cannot be touched with the feeling of our infirmities; but was in all points tempted like as we are, yet without sin." (KJV)* I know this verse by heart. I understood the part about Jesus facing temptation and never giving in. Never sinning. But I guess I was always focused on the action part of sinning, how Jesus never gave in to the temptation to hurt someone or dishonor His mom or lie. But the beginning of the verse says in black and white that it's about feelings, too. Not just not hurting someone, but not being angry with them either. Not just the temptations to acts of sin, but the temptations that come from feelings. "Feelings of our infirmities" to be exact.

If you have chronic health problems, when you're having a flare-up or are in deep pain, you are not likely struggling with temptations toward acts of sin like stealing or gossiping or lust (though I am tempted toward gluttony as my steroids make me VERY hungry). The temptations are inward ones. To fear, to worry, to give in to anxiety or anger or even bitterness. The temptation to envy people who are healthy.

Jesus says He understands. He knows what it is like to feel physical fatigue and pain, much more so than you or I ever will, and all the inward temptations that come with both. He was tempted to fear, to worry, even to envy. Yet He did not sin.

Because He knows, and yet did not sin, He can teach us how to face these temptations without sin as well.

So, next time I want to snap at someone at the dinner table, or stay up at night worrying, I can see these feelings for what they are. Not sins yet, but temptations. And like my high priest, who is touched with compassion for pain, I can resist them and overcome them.

To know that Jesus Himself knows, cares, and is not only ready to listen to my infirm feelings, but also to pray for me, that is victory already!

It's like my fear of flying, a very inconvenient fear considering I've traveled to over twenty countries and been on more than one flight that was eighteen hours with no stops. I am an inward wreck in an airplane, especially if there's turbulence. I hate turbulence. Once, we hit a patch of turbulence so rough, my husband's drink was literally jumping out of his cup. I sat there watching his calm demeanor, thinking I was such a failure because I didn't have his level of faith.

However, for one, I have recognized that a lot of my "fear" is propelled by physical symptoms of getting air sick, like breaking out in a cold sweat and other things that feel akin to panic. For another, and most importantly, the fact of the matter is that every single time I still get on the plane. I may fight the feelings of fear each time we ascend, but I still step onto that flying machine. My actions declare I believe the plane will take me to my destination without crashing. My actions prove what I truly believe. Not my feelings.

This is true with my health as well. What I feel changes, often. My feelings cannot be trusted as the defining factor of my faith or lack of faith in God. What shows my true belief is my actions.

When my condition flares up, and the familiar group of feelings come hurtling toward me, I tend to already see myself as having failed. The feelings are here; I blew it. Thanks to that verse, though, from now on I will try to see this scenario differently. I will see that the feelings arriving are temptations. If I let them come in and take over, fueling actions, then I am sinning and I have failed. If, however, I choose to reject them and instead focus on truth, I have won over them. I am not a city broken down without walls after all.

If you have felt burdened down by the feelings that attack you when you are sick or in pain, be encouraged. Jesus understands how you feel. He's been there. He knows what it is like to face the feelings of infirmities. If you let Him, He will face yours with you, praying for you all the way.

*Who is he who condemns? It is Christ
who died, and furthermore is also risen,
who is even at the right hand of God, who
also makes intercession for us.*

Romans 8:34

Individual or Group Study Questions

1. What emotions tend to come your way when you feel physically awful?

2. What kind of situation brings the most feelings of your infirmities? Sickness, hospitalization, misunderstanding by others, doctors appointments, pain? Describe your biggest battleground when it comes to being tempted with wrong feelings.

3. Do you believe temptation can be toward emotional sins not just actions sins? Why or why not?

4. Are you like me and always considered that the feelings arriving meant you had already failed?

5. How does it make you feel to read that Jesus is touched by the feelings of our infirmities and that He understands?

6. Have you ever thought about the fact that, if you are God's child, Jesus prays for you? What does that mean to you?

7. Do you believe our actions define what we truly believe, rather than our feelings? Why or why not?

8. Why are feelings not to be trusted?

ACTIVITY: Today, talk with God about the feelings of your infirmities. Try to think through a time when Jesus would have struggled with the same feelings you are struggling with right now. Talk through how Jesus responded to that temptation and ask God to show you how you should respond.

CHAPTER THREE

NOT ENOUGH FAITH?

"Rabbi, who sinned, this man or his parents, that he was born blind?" Jesus answered, "Neither this man nor his parents sinned, but that the works of God should be revealed in him."
John 9:2-3

The man approached and sat next to me. "Can I ask you a question?" His tone was serious, his eyes intense.

I had just finished speaking to his small group, talking mostly about human trafficking and how I came to be an author after leaving the mission field. Weaved through that story, however, was an important truth, the truth that God doesn't always fix things the way we expect.

Apparently, this man did not agree with my perspective that God had a purpose in allowing Addison's Disease, hypoglycemia, asthma and a cyst on my brain to bring me home from missions and completely re-route my life.

"Look at this verse," he said, directing me to a Bible passage he believed meant that if I just resisted the sickness (because according to him all sickness could only be from the devil), it would have to flee. He asked me, "Do you believe God *wants* people to be sick?" Then he stared me down, waiting for me to…what? Call out defeat on my health problems, forcing them away by my will so he would be proven correct?

It's hard living with chronic health problems, and harder still when well-meaning friends (or random strangers) imply our problems are somehow our own fault. This is not a new problem—Job's friends did it thousands of years ago and people have been doing variations thereof ever since.

I cannot quite understand the idea some have that God wants our lives happy and free of problems when John 16:33 very clearly says that believers will have tribulation in this life. If having problems is a sign of a lack of faith, then Joseph, Paul, John the Baptist and especially Jesus would need to repent.

When I hear someone implying my illness would go away if only I believed enough or prayed enough, etc., I tend to want to re-question everything. Is this my fault? Am I doing something wrong? I know I fully believe God could heal me at any moment if He chose to, but what if, really deep down, I don't *really* believe it?

Are our sicknesses our own fault? Do we not have enough faith?

Those are heavy questions to carry around, added burdens tacked upon the burden of sickness we already carry.

However, there is one story in the Bible which reminds me that God does not see the way man sees and I don't have to either.

In John 11, Lazarus, a good friend of Jesus, is sick. You probably know the story, but you may have never considered how several facets of it have significant applications for us and our health conditions.

1. Both of Lazarus' sisters, Mary and Martha, had faith—enough faith—that Jesus could heal their brother.

Their level of faith had nothing to do with why Lazarus died.

2. Jesus not only knew about the problem, He cared about the people involved. Even so, He *did not* come.

3. Jesus allowed Lazarus to remain sick and even to die. He could have stopped it at any point, but He chose not to. This choice had nothing to do with the faith or lack of faith of any person involved.

4. Jesus said that

> a. Him waiting despite being needed

> b. Lazarus' death itself

> c. Him showing up "too late"

were not at all a punishment on Lazarus or Mary or Martha. All of the above were for eternal reasons: the glory of God and so many would believe.

5. Jesus wept. Even when He knew He could and would restore Lazarus, Jesus cared about the temporary suffering of those He loved and He cried with them.

I get such peace from this story. It takes my physical health problems and the emotional struggles that come with them, and places them into a beautiful place: the potential for God's glory, the potential for others to believe.

Jesus cares about my suffering and yours. Though He has allowed it for some reason, He hurts with us and He wants to use us to show Himself to the world. Yes, sometimes sickness is a result of sin, and dealing with the sin releases people from the sickness it caused. Also yes, sometimes God provides miraculous healing and gets glory through that. However, sometimes He allows sickness to remain because He has a different plan, one that isn't clear to others and often ourselves, but if we trust Him—if we keep the faith others think we do not have—we will one day see how He is being glorified and will be glorified through us and our pain. In the end, our level of faith isn't about something that others can tangibly grasp, measurable by our health or wealth or abilities. Faith is something only God can measure, and what does reveal our faith to others, according to the Scriptures, are our works for Him (James 2), and some days our greatest work of faith may be enduring hardship as a good soldier of Jesus Christ (2 Timothy 2:3). Other days it may be responding in grace to those people who tell us we're sick because we don't have enough faith (Rom. 12:14).

I don't know how God plans to use my sickness or your sickness, but the how doesn't matter. Just knowing that illness can be part of His plan—rather than because of my lack of faith—gives me, and hopefully you, great comfort today.

The sisters sent to Him,
saying, "Lord, behold, he whom You
love is sick." When Jesus heard that, he
said, "This sickness is not unto death, but
for the glory of God, that the Son of God
may be glorified through it."
John 11:3-4

Individual or Group Study Questions

1. Have you ever had someone tell you your sickness is your own fault?

2. Do people sometimes imply if you just had more faith, your sickness would be healed? How do you feel when people insinuate—or come right out and say—such things?

3. It's hard not to be defensive when your faith is questioned, isn't it? In the story of Lazarus' death, Jesus' love was questioned. Instead of getting defensive and arguing, He used the circumstance to show even more love. Can we use these circumstances to show even more faith through our sickness than we could have if we were miraculously made well?

4. Why do you think Jesus wept?

5. If Jesus was standing next to you when someone accused you of not having enough faith, what do you think He would say to that person?

6. Can you think of other times in Scripture when people had the wrong idea about faith and why bad things happen?

7. Do you believe God could have a grand purpose in your sickness? That your illness could bring Him glory and cause others to believe?

ACTIVTY: Today when you pray, give over to God those who want to decide why you are sick. If you still struggle with wondering if your illness is your own fault, talk to God about that. Are you right with Him? If you are, then get into His Word and ask Him to show you times when He allowed suffering for a higher purpose. Sometimes those with the most faith had the most difficulties! Ask Him to show you a verse you can memorize to renew your own mind and heart when others accuse or imply you don't have enough faith.

CHAPTER FOUR

WHY DIDN'T JESUS HEAL EVERYBODY?

*All of us need to treasure anything within us that makes us feel just
a little detached from the greater arena of human experience, for it
may be the one thing that God mercifully gives us to tie us to Himself
and fill our need to be known by Him.*
Jennifer Rothschild[iii]

When I was growing up, one thing in the Bible never made sense to me. Why would Jesus heal people, but then command them not to tell anyone? Why didn't He tell them to spread the word so He could heal everyone? Was He being stingy with His miracles? I knew He wasn't tired.

It puzzled me very much. I didn't understand this part of God. I knew He was compassionate, but if He was, why didn't He help everyone who was in need? Why didn't He fix it?

After college I moved to Bangladesh for two years, a place with culture still much like that of Bible times. Living there, so many things in the Bible became clear because I watched them happen with my own eyes. Like how scandalous it was that Jesus talked with the woman at the well. Or how easy it would be for the mob to be shouting "Hosanna!" when Jesus arrived, but three days later to be shouting "Crucify Him!" Like how a corrupt tax collector could enslave people and make himself rich. Why Proverbs talks so often about not taking bribes.

In Bangladesh, beggars and street kids were a daily sight. People were in need, hungry, destitute, sick. Sick with illnesses we never see here in America. Untreated tumors that grew into huge bulges, deforming bodies, missing limbs, men crippled into begging for their livelihood, untreated cancer, blindness, skin rashes . . . so many needs. So much hopelessness.

The plight of the street kids burdened me the most. I wanted to rescue them, help them, provide for them. I longed to give. But I learned quickly that giving was a sure way of drawing a crowd, but not a crowd interested in the gospel—a crowd interested in free food. More and more people would come, fighting and clamoring, not for their eternal needs, but the hunger of the moment.

I saw this firsthand when I foolishly took just one package of cookies to a village and got mobbed when I tried to give them out. Had I brought twenty packages, it would not have been enough. Even if I had been able to afford and carry enough for the whole village, it would only have fed them for a moment. What about their supper, or the hunger that would return the following day? Temporary needs are just that—temporary, and meeting them is only a temporary fix.

With our health, how many times has God healed us of sickness, taken away our symptoms, given us relief? Yet right now what feels big and important is our current suffering. We want today's pain fixed, and if God did fix it, we would be grateful until tomorrow's pain came, and then we'd want that fixed, too.

God wants us to have a higher perspective than the hunger of the moment (Col. 3:2). The Israelites experienced this with the manna. Even though God rained food down from the sky, some still worried about not having enough, and complained when the hunger struck again. Even though God daily provided enough for their bodies, it was never enough for their hearts. God wanted their trust and their faith, but even when He was providing their daily needs in a miraculous way, they still could not get past their hunger for more.

Jesus talked about this in the New Testament. After He fed the five thousand, He told the crowd plainly that they were not following because they sought the kingdom of God, but because they sought more food.

It was the same when He healed. Jesus chose to heal individuals, and sometimes He looked with compassion on the multitudes and healed huge masses of people in need, but He knew people's hearts. He knew healing everyone would be an easy ticket to personal fame, but not fulfill why He came.

If healing people, or giving food, or meeting any physical, temporal need, meant crowds would follow Jesus for what Jesus could do for them rather than seeking the kingdom of God, then those things became a deterrent to Jesus' ultimate purpose on earth. He came to heal our souls. Healing bodies was good, just like feeding people was good, but not if it distracted people from their greater need of salvation.

Perhaps that is one of the reasons why God has not healed those of us who live with chronic illness. He has a higher purpose than us feeling comfortable and whole again here on this earth. His gospel is not about health and wealth. Rather, it often requires sacrifice here in this life. If that sacrifice fulfills God's ultimate purpose, is it not better to be sick than to be well? Our choice to honor Him and glorify Him when He doesn't fix it is more testimony to the world than were we all better and back to living life the way we want.

One day all of God's children—every person who has accepted Jesus as Savior—will be healed of everything that binds us in this life. Our time here will seem such a small, insignificant season. In heaven, we will not mind having been sick here on earth it if meant representing our God well, if we lived the truth of His power, not just to make the bad go away, but to uphold and strengthen within the bad.

Be comforted in knowing there is purpose in your pain, and share that comfort with others.

For our light affliction, which is but for a moment, is working for us a far more exceeding and eternal weight of glory.
2 Corinthians 4:17

Individual or Group Study Questions

1. Have you ever wondered why Jesus didn't just heal everybody? Did it feel like Jesus was selfish or unkind?

2. Now that you have read this chapter, does it make a little more sense why Jesus would be secretive about healing sometimes?

3. If you had something great to offer, but everyone was only clamoring for the lesser thing you could provide, what would you do? How would you try to get them to see the greater thing?

4. Do you think your faith through sickness can show people the "greater thing," what they need more than just comfort in this life? How?

5. Are you willing to be that example to the world? What is hard about this? Do you think this is what Jesus is asking of you?

ACTIVITY: Talk with God about His purpose for your personal suffering. Ask Him if He wants to use your sickness to show His power (by healing you) or to show His loving presence (by being with you through your illness rather than making it better). Ask Him to show you the right perspective to have about this difficult calling of living with suffering. Then decide if you are willing to follow that calling with joy.

CHAPTER FIVE

THE ANNOYING VOICE
INSIDE MY HEAD

If your time ain't come not even a doctor can kill you.
American Proverb[iv]

I'm not one for picturing a miniature angel and a miniature devil battling it out on each of my shoulders. I do, however, imagine this little force in my head. You know, the one that nags and whines, the one that mentally pokes with statements like:

It's not fair.

I have the right to be angry.

Everybody else is healthy.

No one has it as bad as me.

No one understands.

If I listen to this little guy and begin focusing on such things, I start wallowing in this yucky mental mud that pulls me in like quicksand. The farther I sink, the harder it is to get back out of the sludge.

John Bunyan called it the "Slough of Despond" in his famous book, *Pilgrim's Progress*. I like that word: slough. It sounds like a blob, and I feel like I'm rolling around in it when I focus on the bad stuff.

For a little while, I actually feel better there. Know what I mean? It feels good to throw yourself a pity party and decide everything in the world is against you, and you have it so bad, and you can't do what you used to do, and God is being mean to you so why should you praise Him at all anymore? Nothing is good, everything is bad . . . think I'll go eat worms.

Most of us know getting to that point is not helpful. Unfortunately, it's possible to get to that point without realizing it, because we were just emotionally responding to that annoying voice in our heads, listening to it and soaking in the wrong thoughts fed to us. We didn't intend to go there; it just happened. We weren't really thinking.

That's the problem. We weren't thinking; we were feeling. We did not purposefully choose what to focus on, and that's a dangerous way to live. The more vulnerable we are, the more dangerous it is.

It's kind of like a woman unhappy in her marriage reading romance novels. She starts using the novels as a kind of emotional pornography, getting her romance needs met somewhere outside her husband. The novels focus on the first feelings of love, feelings the wife misses. Over time, the more she focuses on these unreal men and their created-by-a-female-author tender responses, loving words, and passionate feelings, the more she draws away and eventually despises her own husband.

In the beginning it feels like it helps, but in the end it will lead to the destruction of her marriage relationship.

We all need to be just as careful about what we feed our minds as we are about what we feed our bodies. A good rule is the Philippians 4:8 test, which says we should think on things that are true, noble, just, pure, lovely, virtuous, praiseworthy, and of good report. These are the things we are to focus on. That takes purpose.

I'm not good at remembering that whole list, but it's easy to remember one or two. When I catch myself focusing on something that I can feel eating away at my spirit, I can ask myself, "Is it true?" Sometimes the bad stuff, yes, is true. But then the next question, "Is it lovely?" defines whether that truth is something good to focus on or not.

Like that woman with her novels. It was probably true that her husband wasn't treating her with the loving attention he should. But dwelling on that truth was not lovely, or noble, or pure. Dwelling on it gave her an excuse to decide all the problems in her marriage were because of her husband's failures, and therefore it was not her responsibility to contribute any effort into restoring their relationship.

One great question, one that is very important to those of us who battle the it's-not-fair feeling is, "Is it beneficial?" 1 Corinthians 10:23 says that all things are lawful for us because of grace, but not all things are beneficial. He was speaking of what food to eat and not eat. I think it should apply to the food we feed out minds as well.

This verse is not easy to swallow sometimes (pun intended). For me, it meant stopping something that went into my mouth and affected my mind—i.e. going off caffeine. Completely.

I didn't want to. I really like caffeine. I like the way it clears my mind and helps me focus. It gives me an energy I don't usually have with my adrenal problem. I used to love loading up on it and then getting a big pile of work done and feeling so good while doing it.

That can't be bad, can it?

I'm certainly not going to say that drinking caffeine is a sin. However, for me, it had some important negative ramifications. It affected my insulin, and my body was easily addicted to it. If I drink caffeine more than three days in a row, I start having withdrawal symptoms, mainly terrible headaches.

Then I'd have to drink more to deal with the headaches, which would feel great for a few hours, then I'd feel terrible after that. I started noticing a pattern in my patience level with my children and my constant thinking about when I was going to get some more caffeine.

It was definitely not beneficial to me or my family. I knew I had to stop. I'd try and try to just be moderate about it. What if I just drank one glass a day? One a week? One just on special occasions?

Apparently, I have little capacity for moderation. I heard a guy once say that being 100% about something is easier than 95% because you're always looking for that little 5%. He's right. I finally realized the only way that would be beneficial was going off completely.

It was hard to do. I wanted to give in so much at the beginning. But it got easier over time, and now a lot of times I don't even think about it anymore. I have not had one caffeinated drink in over three years. (I sound like a recovered addict, which I guess I am. That feels weird.)

Being 100% really is easier than 95%. Now that I am committed to absolutely no caffeine, I don't focus on it every time I go out, wondering if it would be okay this time, or next time, or when it's my birthday, or… or… or…

In this same way, we can unwittingly begin to focus ourselves onto something that, even it if is true, is not beneficial, like allowing ourselves to dwell on how it's not fair. We can't trust ourselves to always be thinking rightly (wouldn't it be nice if we could!), and therefore need to take every thought into captivity (2 Cor. 10:5). By doing this, consciously deciding what to focus on, we renew our minds (Rom. 12:2) and in doing so we are transformed.

How does this idea play out in real life? Check out the Bible study companion to this book!

The little voice in our heads is never going to leave for good in this life. But we can tune it out, making that voice smaller as God's voice gains volume. We can take those bad thoughts into captivity, reject them, and replace them with what is true and lovely.

Little voice, be gone!

And let the peace of God rule in your hearts…and be thankful.

Colossians 3:15

Individual or Group Study Questions

1. Of the following phrases, which one hits you the most often?

    a.   It's not fair.

    b.   You have the right to be angry.

    c.   Everybody else is healthy.

    d.   No one has it as bad as you.

    e.   No one understands.

2. When those phrases do hit, are you more likely to feel:

    a.   Angry?

    b.   Discontent?

    c.   Self-pitying?

    d.   Bitter?

3. Do you think the illustration about the woman reading romance novels is a good one? Can you describe how you may have done something like this regarding your health?

4. Can you think of a habit/food/activity/perspective that is not beneficial? Are you willing to change or quit for the good of your health and your walk with the Lord?

5. For you, is 100% better than 95% or not? What do you see as best for you? Why?

6. Which two words in the Philippians 4:8 list stand out as the most significant to you? Why?

ACTIVITY: If there is something you need to change, list the ways that change would be good. Also list reasons why not changing is not beneficial. Put the list on your refrigerator or someplace prominent to help you remember why change is worth it.

CHAPTER SIX

GOD I'LL TRUST YOU IF . . .

The eye of the great Father, fixed mightily on all his children,
rests most tenderly on the couch of the restless sufferer.
Charlotte Bickersteth[v]

We had just arrived in Indonesia, where my husband would teach English as a Second Language at a university on the island of Borneo. I was excited but very tired, which was normal considering the jet-lag caused by a nearly twelve-hour time change from our usual American schedules.

We started out busy, spending the days with our teammates looking for houses, trying the food (fried rice on the yummy side, fish heads on the not-so-yummy side) and getting to know the area. I remember one morning I felt bone-weary. What was wrong with me? Why couldn't I keep up?

Later that day, I was exploring the Indonesian version of a grocery store when I got shaky, clammy, and nearly passed out. It was like a major sugar low, but I hadn't missed a meal or eaten something I shouldn't.

Day after day, these strange symptoms were erratic and unusual. Long story short, I found out I was pregnant. Surprise! I sat in my room staring at that thin pink line on the little stick, slightly jittery on the outside and very jittery on the inside.

I was excited. I was happy.

I was scared.

The control freak who packs weeks in advance for things was pregnant in a third-world country, with no knowledge of the local medical care and pretty much no knowledge of pregnancy.

And I was sick. I had the "normal" pregnancy stuff, but the hard thing was how the pregnancy affected my other health problems, especially my blood sugar. I'm not sure what those hormones were doing, but instead of eating every four hours like I used to, I had to eat every two hours to keep even somewhat stable. Protein bars and such were not available, so I made a lot of tuna fish sandwiches. (I think once we returned to the US I didn't eat tuna fish for months!) Tuna fish sandwiches and grilled cheese sandwiches every two hours for months…it's no wonder I gained fifty pounds.

We found out there was a missionary-run hospital we could go to via a tiny five-seater airplane. Oh my. The day came and I, always an adventure lover, climbed aboard for my very first pregnancy appointment. We flew over the jungle to a small clearing with an even smaller runway. I was going to need to eat right when we landed.

Unfortunately, we got caught in some kind of updraft just as the pilot was about to land and he had to fly up and circle to try again. Pregnancy, sugar low, and circling in the air do not make a happy combination. By the time we finally arrived, I was shaking and had to drink some orange juice.

About thirty minutes later, right when the ultrasound technician started looking at my tiny three-months-along baby, that OJ kicked in. "I don't believe this! I've never seen anything like this!" she said.

Not exactly what you want to hear when someone's looking at your child. "What is it?"

She let me see and my heart soared. Instead of a little tiny lump of sleeping baby, my miniature son was kicking and rolling and flipping around, having a great time with the sugar I'd given him. It was one of the most precious things I had ever seen.

We returned home to face a few months of worrying over placenta previa, some bleeding and cramping, and a lot of fear on my part. We couldn't afford to keep flying back there, so were pretty much on our own when it came to that pregnancy, a fact which didn't sit well with me at all. My body wasn't normal, so this pregnancy wasn't normal, and we didn't have any normal healthcare available anyway!

I did a lot of praying during those months. I remember telling God things like, "I'd trust You if we had some kind of good medical care," or, "I'd trust You if there was some resource for an emergency." I begged God for help. I prayed He would provide so I would not feel so helpless, so without resources. (Sound familiar? Do you ever catch yourself praying like that when there is a medical crisis, or you're having a flare up, or you're on your way to an appointment but you know the doctors won't know what to do with you?)

And in those days and weeks, God whispered to me that if I was praying, "I'd trust You if," it meant I didn't really trust Him. I was saying I would have faith in God if He fixed everything so I had no need to trust Him, so I was not afraid to put my body and my baby in His hands because I had a backup plan that made me feel secure.

I had to face myself those months, and since. There's a boundary line somewhere in my soul. Anything within that boundary, I can trust God with. But the closer circumstances get to that boundary line, or especially if they cross it, that's too far. Too risky. Too much. I stop trusting God and start asking (whining, pleading, begging) Him to change the circumstances until they are back within the boundary of my ability to trust Him.

God wants us to have no boundaries when it comes to trusting Him. It is impossible to do so, humanly speaking. It is impossible to trust God with the impossible, with the truly frightening, with the incomprehensible.

And yet, God reaches to us where we are and nudges us toward those boundaries of trust. He asks us to cross the line. He leads us to walk with Him through the unanswered questions, allowing Him to replace our fears with a peace that doesn't make any sense (Phil. 4:7).

I would like to say I learned my lesson. That I erased the boundary lines and now run freely across them. The truth is, though, that I still feel them. Anytime I near them I still struggle with handing those things over to God and letting Him be in charge, believing, truly believing He will do what is best.

When I am afraid, I remember that time of pregnancy and fear. I felt like we were unsafe because of the circumstances. God showed me that safety is of the Lord (Ps. 4:8). When my little boy was born, the doctor said God must have been protecting him because he had a knot in his umbilical cord that she couldn't figure out how food got through. All those outward circumstances I feared, and the greatest threat was within my own body, something I was completely helpless to fix.

So, when I'm tempted to tell God, "I'd trust You if," He reminds me of all the times He has taken me past that boundary line of security, and still taken care of me. I don't know that I'll ever be able to walk over there comfortably, but I know I can walk there confidently, because safety is of the Lord. As long as I'm holding His hand, there is no need to fear.

Whenever I am afraid,
I will trust in You.
Psalm 56:3

Individual or Group Study Questions

1. Have you ever caught yourself praying, "God I'll trust You if..."? What was your "if" about?

2. What in your life do you find hardest to hand over to God?

3. Do you believe God wants what is best for you? Why or why not?

4. Do you believe safety is of the Lord? Why or why not?

5. Have you ever had a time you really feared something, and come to find out the danger was in a totally different place? What happened?

6. Have you ever had a time where there was danger you did not even know about, but God took care of you? Did that affect the way you see God's presence in your life?

7. What do you think it would take for you to be able to trust God with everything?

ACTIVITY: Today, talk with God about the things you fear trusting Him with. Tell Him why. Ask Him to show you a time when He was taking care of you through something you could neither control nor fix yourself. Ask Him to show you this week that He is watching over you.

ILLNESS AND DEPRESSION

He does not call on the feeble to march with the flock, but simply to submit to be carried. If the tempter tries to goad you even there, do not turn round to look on him, but hide your head deeper in your Savior's bosom.
Charlotte Bickersteth[vi]

I don't like this topic. In fact, I'd really prefer to throw this chapter in the trash. However, there is enough of a connection between depression and chronic illness that I cannot pretend I am the only one to have experienced it.

It all started a little over halfway through my two years serving in South Asia, in one of the poorest countries of the world. The pain and suffering all around me touched me deeply. Being empathetic in nature is a gift, but carries with it a weakness.

I would suffer through monsoon season, hating that I was warm and dry while so many lived on the streets with no covering. Some days I did not want to walk out the door, wanting to avoid seeing maimed street kids, beggars carrying hungry babies, children scrounging through the trash looking for used paper to sell, or adults doing the same looking for a bite of food to soften the never-ending sting of hunger.

I also encountered culture shock, which is a time period in a new cultural setting where the newness has worn off, the differences are more bothersome than exciting, and a person begins to feel that all they want is to return to what is comforting and secure and "normal" to them. (I believe we all go through a kind of culture shock after a year or two of being unhealthy, wanting to go back to the way our lives used to be and hating the adjustments we continue to have to make.)

To top it off, I had some habits that were negatively affecting not only my physical condition, but my emotional condition as well. Being a night person, I used to love staying up past when everyone else was asleep. Then I would drag through the following day, longing for bedtime until around ten p.m. when my body would suddenly wake up and I would not be able to get to sleep until even later than the previous night.

The first day I realized something was really wrong still stands out in my memory. It was July fourth, and we had a big party scheduled that evening. That morning, I slept past when I should have eaten, and my sugar was crashing so badly I could barely drag myself from my room to ask someone to go find me a Coke©. It seemed to take forever, but finally I was handed one of those old-fashioned glass bottles, still used in Asia, filled with sugary liquid. I drank it quickly and waited for my body to stop shaking.

For any of you who don't have blood sugar problems, suffice it to say that if you start out the day on a sugar crash, your whole day is messed up. I continued preparing for the party, drinking more sugar-filled drinks when my sugar started dropping again. By the time the party started, I did not even want to attend, but I was determined to make it a success.

People arrived, the fun began, and suddenly I was filled with a deep, dark fear. I can't really explain it, but it was terrifying. I tried to ignore it and enjoy the party, but it would not leave me. Quite the opposite. It continued haunting me at the strangest times throughout the following days, and was worst in the long hours of the night when I had no one around to distract my thoughts.

I responded incorrectly. When the feeling came, I dived into it, hoping if I analyzed and studied and focused on it, I could understand where it came from and how to make it go away.

No one knew what I was going through. I was good at faking it. After all, God's children aren't supposed to ever struggle with fear and doubt and depression, right? Especially not one on the mission field. My shame at what I was feeling drove me deeper into myself. I began to even hide away from God, listening to lies that even He was against me.

For six months, I struggled daily with thoughts that terrified me, questions whispered to me by some kind of evil, to the point where I feared I would just lose it completely. I was afraid to be in the house by myself because of the knives in the kitchen. I dreaded a lifetime of struggling against something I did not even understand. And I felt very alone.

Dear friend, if you are reading this with tears in your eyes because you know exactly what I am talking about, you are the reason I am telling this story now. I'm not faking it anymore. I have learned that holding darkness inside and never sharing your struggles only makes the evil more powerful. I don't want you to go through this alone, and neither does God.

Now that I am out of that dark tunnel, I can look back and see some important contributing factors that are worth sharing:

1. I was listening to lies. God was not the One telling me life was hopeless and had no point. God was not filling me with the spirit of fear. I was listening to lies that told me this was a spiritual failure, that I shouldn't tell anyone, that I should pretend I was fine, that God was not good after all.

2. I made the problem worse by focusing on the darkness. By spending hours and days and months living deep within myself, I gave the depression more power.

3. My health problems were affecting my emotions. The problem began more as a result of physical problems rather than spiritual ones. I did not recognize that at the time, and thus did not deal with the bad health habits I had, assuming the depression was entirely a spiritual problem.

4. I did not get help. For months I was too afraid or too ashamed or too proud to admit I was struggling and ask for help. I used to think I was humble because I thought so lowly of myself. God convicted me, however, with the truth that if I'm beating myself up all day, that's actually inverted pride, because **even negative self-absorption is still self-absorption.**

5. I tried to fight the problem with my own reason and my emotions as the defining factor instead of clinging to the Word of God and letting His truth set me free.

It actually took several years before I realized that the time of depression was more based on my body rather than my soul. During those years, I lived with a fear of it happening again (and as I felt helpless against it, that fear was legitimate). The truth came out when I got pregnant for the first time.

Pregnancy drastically affected my health for the worse. I felt horrible. Then that phase hit where I had to go to the bathroom all the time, even in the middle of the night. I would wake up, and immediately that same pattern of dark thoughts attacked me. It scared me. One night, though, I realized this was the same exact pattern of depression thoughts I had experienced years ago. I realized the thoughts were coming during my physically weak times, when I was also weaker emotionally—a recipe for depression.

From that moment, I had the truth, and the truth set me free. I am more than my emotions. I do not have to feel trapped by them anymore. Now instead, I cling to the promise of a sound mind in 2 Timothy 1:7.

God wants us to live in the light. He knows that darkness is a terrifying, lonely place. When we come into the light, even as it exposes our struggles, we can be free.

Here's the conclusion of the matter: chronic illness wears down the body, which wears down the emotions. We as chronically ill people need to understand that our emotions are vulnerable just as our bodies are. We need to protect our emotions, just as we work to protect our health. That means attacking the wrong thoughts with truth, just as we attack bacteria with medication. We also need to change habits that feed the wrong feelings—as the Bible says, "Let us pursue the things which make for peace" (Rom. 14:19). God wants our lives filled with peace, not fear.

(Side Note: For certain health conditions or medications, depression is a symptom/side effect that is not due to habits or thoughts that can be personally overcome, and should not be ignored. For example, I've been told that people who have had their thyroid removed struggle with depression. There is a reason for that: their bodies' hormones are imbalanced and depleted and some are gone entirely. Just as a body missing an electrolyte needs it provided through an outside source, such as a pill, so some people need the resource of medication to give their minds and bodies the depression-fighting capabilities they need. That is completely different than popping a pill because someone is ignoring unresolved issues or just wanting an escape. A body that is missing depression-fighting chemicals or hormones cannot produce them by will or desire, any more than will or desire can make my faulty adrenal glands suddenly start producing cortisol again.

If the truth is that you need medication to stave off depression, then you need it. Give yourself permission to not feel badly about that, or feel defined by it.)

Whether you are genetically inclined toward depression, personality inclined toward depression, or you've never even come close to depression, the truth is that now, with chronic health problems, it is something you need to be prepared to battle. We must learn to live according to the truth, not our feelings. For the truth sets us free.

How did I get past the fear of depression taking over again? I learned during that pregnancy time to fight the feelings not by focusing on them, but by focusing on truth. From the moment I woke, I turned my mind away from those thoughts (I did not start analyzing them but rejected them, like mentally flushing a toilet) and instead quoted Scripture, as I got up and went to the bathroom, until I was back in bed. It was the only thing powerful enough to cover over and replace the dark thoughts.

God's Word is powerful enough to fight any feeling. I do not have to be controlled by my emotions anymore. I have the truth, and the truth has set me free.

It can set you free, too.

.

He also brought me up out of a horrible pit, out of the miry clay, and set my feet upon a rock, and established my steps.
Psalm 40:2

Individual or Group Study Questions

1. Do you think depression is always a spiritual problem? Why or why not?

2. Have you ever experienced a time like this? Do you remember when it started?

3. Can you see any relation between that time and a decline or crisis in your health?

4. Do you think the condition of your body affects the condition of your mind? Explain.

5. What are some lies you have been tempted to believe?

    a.   God is not good.

    b.   God is not good to me.

    c.   Depression is a punishment.

    d.   I deserve this. I'm no good.

    e.   Nothing will change. I will feel like this forever.

    f.   I am helpless against my feelings.

    g.   It's not worth it.

    h.   There is no hope.

6. Have you ever told anyone about your struggles? How did they respond? If you haven't, how do you fear they will respond?

ACTIVITY: Can you think of someone very godly, someone trustworthy who you can talk with when you are struggling? Schedule a time to talk with them when you are feeling strong. Explain everything and ask if they are willing to help you when you are weak. During the strong times, memorize one or several of the verses in the Bible study for this chapter to prepare to fight the darkness the next time it comes.

CHAPTER EIGHT

THE IF ONLYS AND WHAT IFS

God never puts our life on hold. We put our life on hold. Sometimes the very thing that we are allowing to hold us back is what God has allowed in our lives to move us forward.
Jennifer Rothschild[vii]

One of the easiest ways to get worried, depressed and angry is to start walking the trail of If Onlys and What Ifs.

If Onlys tend to live in the realm of the past and present.

The Past:

If only I hadn't had that accident.

If only the doctor hadn't made that mistake.

If only I'd known what the problem was sooner.

The Present:

If only I could get a decent night's sleep. (Amen!)

If only it wasn't so hard to explain.

If only there was some cure, some medication, something to help.

If only my spouse/mother/friends/siblings were more helpful or understanding.

What Ifs tend to cloud our future.

The Future:

What if I get sick the day of that big event?

What if there's an emergency when I'm alone?

What if this never gets better?

What if I'm really dying?

All of the above boil down to one word: trust. Most of us have officially declared Jesus Christ our Savior. We have asked Him to forgive our sins and give us heaven.

But when it comes to handing over our lives, our days, our present circumstances and yes, even our health, we may have never actually handed those over to Him. (Or, if you're like me, you have the bad habit of taking them back to worry over them again!) We say we trust God, but most of the time we say that when things feel in control.

Do we really trust God? Enough to believe that even our health problems are part of His great purpose? Enough to stop complaining about them as some random thing that happened to us, and see them as a useful tool in God's kingdom? Enough to choose peace in the midst of pain?

That is a very hard thing to do. It's even harder when we are thinking on the What Ifs and If Onlys. And we can make it even more difficult when our habits and choices keep us walking on the What If and If Only path.

Say you used to love running marathons, but now you can't anymore because of your condition. You miss running. You think about how wonderful it felt to run. You spend a good part of your day remembering the past, when you used to run and all the wonderful things that came with it. If only you could still run. If only God had given you some other limitation.

You get involved with a group of people who run marathons, because they're fun to hang out with and you get some of that old feeling back.

But when the shot goes off and all those people run toward the finish line, leaving you behind, you feel the terrible loss over and over again. You feel it and you focus on it. It's not fair. Your life is over. You end up either complaining about what a victim you are, or bitterly blaming the doctors or the sickness or even God, or you push even harder into the running world as an outlet for your anger.

Having a condition has changed more than just your body. The world around you may not have changed (people shouldn't stop running marathons because you can't anymore), but you need to change your place in it.

In the beginning, as you grieve and try to accept your loss, it would probably be a good idea to stop hanging out with the marathon group for awhile. Stop watching races on TV. You need a separation from the person you used to be, and time to pray and decide what new direction your life is going to take, because it is unwise to stop a major focus and leave it empty. That can make the If Onlys even worse.

Because of your love for racing, maybe you could join another group, a group of people who race in wheelchairs. Hanging out and helping in their races would not only stay in your field of interest, but seeing people overcoming despite their handicap would remind you of good things—like the fact that you can still walk.

I have to be careful about my involvement with people who travel internationally. As much as I would love to go to a conference full of missionaries and jump back into that world of countries and culture and people groups, I know I would struggle with sadness over the fact that I will likely never go overseas again. I think of the past (getting to travel around the world, encountering beautiful, exciting cultures), of the present (just the idea of getting on an airplane again makes my stomach clench) and the future (when my kids are teenagers and want to go on a missions trip, even if it is in America, I likely will not be able to go with them).

Because of that—just typing it brought tears to my eyes—I probably shouldn't surround myself with people who are still doing what I can no longer do. However, I can get involved with the groups that love and support missions here in my area. Most of them have never been overseas and never will, but they have a heart for what God is doing around the world. With them I am regularly reminded of what a gift I have had—a whole lifetime of amazing experiences before my health stopped me. And through my writing and speaking I get to take people on verbal tours to these places and share missions with them in a unique and valuable way.

Do you see how being with the one group makes it harder to stay positive and being with the other makes it easier?

Focus is really what it comes down to. Focus and trust. If I really trust that God has allowed this condition into my life for a reason, then I can move on with the life He has given me now instead of living in the past, in the life I used to have.

If I really trust God, then I don't have to fear the What Ifs either, because He will be just as loving and good years down the road as He has been in the past.

And if you're having a hard time seeing God as loving and good, and therefore having a hard time trusting Him, you're not alone. Gracia Burnham was a missionary who was kidnapped, held hostage for over a year, then at the moment of their big rescue, her husband was shot and killed by the very group supposed to save them.

I heard her speak once and she said a phrase I'll never forget. She talked about how she didn't want to leave the Philippines where they had served. She did not want to be a single mom. She said it was "the death of a dream."

That was right around the time we had finally decided/admitted that we couldn't live overseas any longer because of my health. I was embarrassed at how I sobbed while she spoke. My dream was dying, too.

It's hard to set aside the hopes we had for ourselves, the plans we made, the things we used to be able to do. If only things were different. If only we were still healthy and strong.

But even in these trials there are some benefits. For one, over time through our experiences, we learn to really trust God, even when there are no answers that make sense. Most of all, we learn to know God in a deeper way than those who do not suffer.

Corrie Ten Boom, who was captured for aiding Jews during the Nazi Holocaust, was imprisoned in a concentration camp. Her entire family died. She survived, and God used her testimony of suffering and forgiveness in incredible ways all over the world.

Once she commented that during her time of desperate suffering in that concentration camp, she came to know God in a deeper way than she ever did before or since.

That really struck me. I would have assumed that once she'd come to know God in such a deep way, it would always remain so.

But I have noticed in my own life how I cling to God and His promises and His presence so much more during the times of pain and suffering than I do when life is going smoothly and I feel secure. Don't you?

People who suffer get the blessing of knowing God in a very close way, not because others need Him less, but because those suffering are constantly reminded of that need, which makes suffering, in some mysteriously complex paradox, something beautiful.

I don't have any big answers as to why God has allowed your struggle. However, I do know that God loves you, He is good, and He will be with you through every moment of your pain and loss.

God is trustworthy to do what is best. With our lives, with our futures, with our bodies. We can put the If Onlys and the What Ifs into the palm of His hand. And, if we can let go of them and leave them there, we can move on to the new life He wants for us.

The eternal God is your refuge,
and underneath are the
everlasting arms.
Deuteronomy 33:27

KIMBERLY RAE

Individual or Group Study Questions

1. Of the "onlys," which one do you battle the most?

    a.   If only I hadn't had that accident.

    b.   If only the doctor hadn't made that mistake.

    c.   If only I'd known what the problem was sooner.

    d.   If only I could get a decent night's sleep.

    e.   If only it wasn't so hard to explain.

    f.   If only there was some cure, some medication, something to help.

    g.   If only my spouse/mother/friends/siblings were more helpful or understanding.

2. Of the "ifs," which one do you battle the most?

    a.   What if I get sick the day of that big event?

    b.   What if there's an emergency when I'm alone?

    c.   What if this never gets better?

    d.   What if I'm really dying?

3. Do you have your own What Ifs and If Onlys that come to mind related to your individual situation? List them here.

4. Do you believe all the What Ifs and If Onlys boil down to trust? Explain.

5. Do you think it is possible to have peace even through pain and suffering? Why or why not?

6. Do you agree with the author that, even though the world hasn't changed, you need to change your place in it? Explain.

7. What is something you used to love that is not an option for you now due to your illness? Do you find yourself remaining near it, focusing on it, living in the past regarding it? Do you think that is good?

8. Can you think of a replacement for that former hobby, interest or ability?

9. Share your opinion on the following statement:

. . . If I really trust that God has allowed this condition into my life for a reason, then I can move on with the life He has given me now instead of living in the past, in the life I used to have.

10. Can you see some benefit to your suffering? List any answers below.

ACTIVITY: Can you adapt the old things you used to love into something you can do now with your health limitations? If you think of something, go for it!

Perhaps looking back fills you with sorrow or shame. Some If Onlys need to be dealt with before they can be left behind. If your If Only is regret because of sin, confess that sin and be forgiven (1 John 1:9; Psalm 51). Then you can get rid of it just like God says He does (Psalm 103:12). If it is a wrong choice or habit that has led to some of your health problems, stop doing that habit (Proverbs 26:11) and replace it with a good one.

CHAPTER NINE

HURTING ALONE

You are mine.... I will be with you.
God[viii]

Some of you reading this book suffer not only with chronic illness, but the added pain of suffering alone. You may be physically alone, living in a quiet house with no one there to comfort or help. Or you may be emotionally alone, your illness and symptoms rejected or ignored by those you'd hoped would love and understand you most. You may even be spiritually alone, having no one who shares your faith to remind you to hope in God during the difficult times.

If you are alone, I can only imagine the added burden that is to your life, and I feel a heavy grief for you. God wants us to bear one another's burdens, to lift each other up, to comfort one another. Missing out on giving and receiving those things is missing out on something God intended.

I do not presume to have a magic formula to fix this. I'm not going to tell you to just focus on happy things and get over it, or burden you further by saying you should get out more and find a bunch of friends. No, sometimes there is no easy solution. Sometimes the pain is not the absence of loved ones, but rather their rejection, and that is a wound not quickly healed.

The only thing I can offer is a loved one who never falters for a moment in His love for you. Yes, I'm talking about God. No, I'm not offering a pat answer, a way to ignore your pain. Exactly the opposite. I have learned that the deeper the pain, the more only God can be the answer. Only He truly understands. Only He knows how deep our suffering penetrates.

And yet He, the one who knows our darkest moments of despair, our worst feelings of anger, our biggest temptations to bitterness, He is the one who loves us most.

I could try to elaborate, but instead I hope you don't mind if I tell a story. As I've said before, I'm a visual person, and so God often shows me truth in ways I can see. This truth came through my child, and me...

My two-year-old little boy was having unexplained health problems. They were mostly digestive, and as we lived overseas, my husband and I were concerned about parasites.

When we returned to America, we took our young son to several doctors. The family physician discovered nothing, and our son went up the line until he was looked at by a digestive specialist. This specialist ordered blood tests, meaning my toddler would have to have his blood drawn—not just the finger-poking kind, but the real, needle-in-the-vein kind of blood tests.

I cannot tell you how I dreaded that experience. When the day came, my stomach was in knots. My son walked into the doctor's office as cheerfully as usual, unaware of what was coming. When I sat him on my lap in the black laboratory chair, and held him to me as a nurse plunged that needle deep into his arm, everything changed. His face contorted. He began to cry, to try to get away from the pain, to wail out his confusion at this unexpected injustice.

My heart cried with him every moment until they got all the blood needed for the required tests. I hurt for his physical pain, but even more for the emotional pain he suffered. He, who was sitting in the lap of the one who had kissed his scraped elbows and imagined hurts, was now being held down by that same person, forced to suffer pain.

How could this be? Had I stopped loving him? Did I want to have him go through this terrible thing? Had I forsaken him? I could have stopped it, but I didn't. Why?

Just thinking about his hurt little face and his cries still hurts my heart. Years have passed and he doesn't even remember that day, but I do.

Most adults know the pain of having to take a child through a painful situation rather than enabling them to sidestep it. Sometimes it is because of our own helplessness (like a broken heart or a hope disappointed). Other times it is because the painful experience is for their ultimate good (like a surgery, or medical testing). As much as it hurt me to see my son being hurt, I knew I had to allow him to go through this so we could help him. It was for his ultimate good, but he could not see that during the time of pain. All he knew was that his mother was not fixing the problem; her arms were the ones holding him there.

I could not take away the pain, but I did stay with him. As much as I hated to see what he was going through, I had to suffer it with him. He is mine. I love him. When he hurts, I hurt.

Within that circumstance, I saw a glimpse of my God.

When we go through difficult trials and painful circumstances, one of the first things we question is God's love for us. How could God let this happen? Why doesn't He fix it?

If God really loved us, surely He would take away this problem, wouldn't He?

We live in a world of pain, and God does not keep all that pain from ever touching us. When the difficult times come, however, know this:

1. God is there. He is with you every moment that you suffer (Psalm 46:1).

2. God cares. He loves you so much. His heart hurts when you hurt (Isaiah 49:15-16).

3. God has a purpose in this time. You may never see in this life what that purpose is, but you can be sure there is one. (See the book of Job. God never did tell Job the reason for his suffering, but we know that eternity was watching; what Job was going through had much bigger, spiritual ramifications than he could ever have imagined.)

4. God will work this for good if we love Him and commit to His purpose in us (Romans 8:28).

I could not watch my child suffer without suffering with him. God, a much better parent that I will ever be, declares, "Can a woman forget her nursing child, and not have compassion on the son of her womb? Surely they may forget, yet I will not forget you" (Isaiah 49:15). I cannot imagine turning my back on my son if he were in any kind of pain. How much more so will God never turn away from us when we suffer!

God may not make the pain go away, but He will hold us as we hurt. We can rest in knowing that there is a purpose to be fulfilled, even in suffering, and that we are loved by the greatest Father of all, a Father who says, "I will never leave you nor forsake you" (Hebrews 13:5).

The God of the universe loves you. He sees; He knows; He cares.

You are not alone.

I will never leave you
nor forsake you.
Hebrews 13:5b

Individual or Group Study Questions

1. Do you feel alone? Is your loneliness:

    a.   Physical - there literally isn't anyone there.

    b.   Emotional - the people around you ignore or reject your suffering.

    c.   Spiritual - they don't understand or accept your faith.

2. For you, what is the hardest part of being alone?

3. Do you feel you have to pretend you are fine to those around you? Why or why not?

4. Is there a way to change your circumstances to make things a little easier, or are you "stuck"?

5. Have you talked with God about your situation and your feelings of loneliness? If not, why not?

ACTIVITY: Take some time and read through Psalm 139. Write down how you feel as you read it. Then, write the personal verses out, but insert your name instead of "I" and "he." Place those verses someplace where you can see them every day and remember you are never alone.

CHAPTER TEN

WHEN THE MOUNTAIN WON'T MOVE

Faith does not eliminate questions.
But faith knows where to take them.
Elisabeth Elliot[ix]

Hebrews 11 is a marvelous chapter known to many as the Hall of Faith. The first half of the chapter lists great heroes of the Old Testament. Then verses 33-35a are enough to make us cheer: subduing kingdoms, obtaining promises, stopping lions, escaping fire and sword, victory in battle, and even having the dead brought back to life again.

How did all this happen? *"Through faith,"* says verse 33. The faith that moves mountains.

That faith has not been extinguished over time. Believers still see God do mighty things. Cancer disappears. Alcoholics get deliverance. Battles are won.

But what about us? What about we who are sick, and have been sick for years? We who have prayed and asked and hoped for healing, but not received it?

As I've said and you likely have experienced, some people think our chronic illness or disease is representative of our lack of faith. That we failed in our battle. We lost. If we could only believe more, condemn the sickness, declare ourselves healthy, we would be free.

Those people did not heed the rest of the chapter on faith. Look on, starting right after those believers who had the ultimate visual victory—the dead coming to life again—as a representation of their faith:

"...and others were tortured, not accepting deliverance...

they were stoned, they were sawn asunder,

were tempted, were slain with the sword...

destitute, afflicted, tormented" (Heb. 11:35b-37).

Wait a minute. How can words like afflicted and tormented be in a chapter celebrating faith? Many would say those people didn't have enough faith. If they had, they would have been delivered to live a comfortable and healthy and victorious life, right?

Not according to God. Read on. The chapter ends this way: *"And these all, having obtained a good report through faith..."* (vs. 39).

Sometimes faith results in healing or victory, in what looks to us humans like what faith should look like. Jesus once said if you have enough faith, you can tell a mountain to move and it will (Matthew 17:20). That's a pretty obvious way to show your faith.

Does that mean that people whose mountains move are closer to God, and people who have mountains still in their backyard aren't?

Not necessarily.

I could list many examples in Scripture, but let's go straight to our ultimate example of perfect faith and oneness with God—Jesus Christ.

First, Jesus never told a mountain to move so we could "see" His faith. In fact, He rejected the suggestion when His disciples, skeptics, and even Satan suggested He do an obvious sign to prove Himself to the world. We should take that to heart. Faith shouldn't be about the show.

Second, Jesus prayed a prayer that God said "no" to. Jesus even asked God "why?" Both were during the time of His greatest suffering. Both were during a time when religious people questioned His faith (the faith of the Messiah Himself!) and mocked His lack of "ability" to get off the cross. Both were also on the path to the greatest glory and victory history has ever witnessed.

At one point, Jesus said He could have made the problem go away. He could have instantly summoned legions of angels to deliver Him (Matthew 26:53). They could have taken away His pain. Given Him health and wealth.

Instead, He let the mountain remain. He told God, *"Father, if it is Your will, take this cup away from Me;* **nevertheless** *not My will, but Yours, be done"* (Luke 22:42, emphasis mine).

For some of us, God wants the mountain to remain. Moving it might impress people and make them feel like we have faith, but sometimes it takes more faith to let God be glorified through our suffering rather than being delivered from it.

As in Hebrews, sometimes God is glorified by delivering His children from the trial. Other times, He is glorified by helping them endure it. God has a purpose for each of us individually, and trying to decide why one was delivered from, and another is being delivered through, is faulty. As Paul warns in 2 Corinthians 10:12, "But they, measuring themselves by themselves, and comparing themselves among themselves, are not wise."

I live right at the base of the Blue Ridge Mountains. Those beautiful peaks have been there for millennia, despite the fact that I live in the "Bible Belt" and there are many people with great faith here. Why do they remain? Is it because no one has had enough faith to move them?

Or are they there because God wants them there? They glorify Him to the world. When I see them, I am filled with awe, given peace, reminded by lifting up my eyes to the hills that my help comes from God (Psalm 121).

For some reason, God has chosen not to move my mountain of chronic illness. He has moved many other mountains in my life—I have seen Him do amazing things—but this one He has allowed to remain.

If I love Him, if I care more about His glory than my own comfort (or about convincing people like Job's friends, which is usually a waste of emotion and time), then I will pray like Jesus. I can ask God to move the mountain, remove the suffering, but end that what I want most is for His will to be done, not mine.

Sometimes it takes more faith to not get what we want. That kind shows, but it's a lot like beauty. Sometimes we see someone who is beautiful, but we can't pinpoint it to their lips or eyes or the shape of their nose, or any one feature. (I don't think I've ever seen a beautiful nose, now that I think about it.) They just shine. That's the kind of faith we who live with illness can have. The kind that looks up and is radiant and unashamed (Psalm 34:5). The kind that, like the mountains, others can look to and be comforted.

I love the mountains here in North Carolina. Maybe someday I will even learn to love my illness, if it can show others where their help comes from.

*And this is the victory
that has overcome the world
—our faith.
1 John 5:4*

Individual or Group Study Questions

1. Has anyone ever told you you're not better yet because you don't have enough faith?

2. Have you ever worried that maybe this was true?

3. What do you think is God's perspective on suffering?

4. Where do you think sickness and suffering come from?

    a.   Always from the devil.

    b.   Always from God.

    c.   Could be either or both.

    d.   Neither, it's just chance.

5. If you believe suffering comes from God sometimes, why do you think God sends it?

    a.   To punish.

    b.   To help us grow.

    c.   To help others grow or be comforted.

    d.   To protect us from something bad we'd have pursued otherwise.

    e.   To bring glory to Him through our endurance and faith.

    f.   Any and/or all of the above.

6. Which of the above do you think God is wanting to accomplish through your current sickness?

ACTIVITY: Imagine God and Satan are having a conversation about you, just as they did about Job. What do you think Satan would say to God about where your weak points are? What do you think God would say to Satan about His strength in you? At the end of your life, how would you want their conversation to conclude?

CONCLUSION

FEARFULLY AND WONDERFULLY MADE

Heaven is not here, *it's* There. *If we were given all we wanted here,*
our hearts would settle for this world rather than the next.
God is forever luring us up and away from this one,
wooing us to Himself and His still invisible Kingdom,
where we will certainly find what we so keenly long for.
Elisabeth Elliot[x]

A tiny part of my body does not function correctly. Because of this, I live my life on a strict schedule of pills, pills and more pills, not to mention a special diet, restricted activity, etc. You know the drill.

This morning after a handful of pills, my yucky-tasting liquid medication, and my specialized breakfast, I was thinking of how much effort it took just to replace (or try to replace) the function of one, extremely small part of my body.

Suddenly it was as if the Lord opened my eyes. I was complaining about how much I had to invest in keeping my own body running. But I'm only "helping out" a part that's about the size of my thumbnail. All the rest—the organs, tissues, the millions and millions of cells—God's been keeping all that running every moment of every day my entire life.

"The human body is comprised of billions of microscopic units, each with their own unique function yet all working together to create one smoothly operating entity,"[xi] says Dr. Peter Abrahams in *How The Body Works*. Each human body has over 200 bones, over 600 muscles, 10 trillion cells, and over 100,000 hairs (well, most of us anyway).

The heart pumps over 1,500 gallons of blood each day, beating 100,000 times. Each of us breathes thousands of times per day, most of those breaths taken without conscious thought.

Imagine if we had to tell ourselves to breathe each moment, tell our hearts to beat, consciously blink our eyelids, digest our food, see, hear, taste. And don't forget the mind. Can you imagine having to process and store the thousands of thoughts that come to mind each day?

Millions of things are functioning within each of our bodies all day long without any effort on our part.

Maybe we are looking at things backwards. Instead of asking why things aren't as good as they "should" be, why don't we ask why things are as good as they are?

Why do our bodies function at all?

Why can we wake up each morning and breathe without even trying?

Why do our hearts keep beating without us telling them to?

God is keeping my body going every moment of every day. But most of the time, I don't even think about it, until something doesn't work the way it should, and I start complaining.

Perhaps God has allowed my health problems to remind me how much of me He has taken responsibility to keep going, showing me how much I have to be thankful for, and indeed how little I have to complain about.

Life is a gift, and every part of our bodies that works is a gift. I start to consider how life would be if I had to be responsible for 40 or 50 or 100 of the millions of things happening to keep my body functioning. When I look at it that way, suddenly instead of complaining, I feel thankful that I only have to keep track of 20 or so!

Therefore, this day that the Lord has made, I will try to take my pills and do my routine with a joyful heart, thankful that I'm not in charge of all my organs and cells and a million other things God is doing for me.

God says I am fearfully and wonderfully made (Psalm 139:14). It's time I did more than just say I believe that. It's time I lived like it, too.

Will you join me?

But we have this treasure

in earthen vessels,

that the excellence of the power

may be of God and not of us.

We are hard-pressed on every side,

yet not crushed;

we are perplexed,

but not in despair;

persecuted, but not forsaken;

struck down,

but not destroyed.

2 Corinthians 4:7-9

Who is this God?

In all my travels, I have encountered many different people with many different beliefs. I once was shown a site where animal sacrifices were performed to the gods, and the guide proudly told me that in the past they also offered sacrifices that were human. I've watched people present plates of food to statues, food that should have gone to hungry children. I've seen a tree covered with colored strings representing the prayers of thousands. I've seen supposedly sacred monkeys, sacred cows, and cursed turtles.

I've smelled the incense and heard the gongs and felt the desolation of the millions who seek to get attention from a god or gods who have no compulsion to care, who must be bribed and appeased as motivation to answer prayers or help a suffering worshipper.

I also have dear friends who follow a religion which claims that if they miss one prayer time, they must suffer many years in hell, yet they do miss prayers, so do they truly believe? Or do they hope that it won't really matter in the end, that whoever is in charge is not paying attention, or won't really care?

If you read about religions, you will find gods and goddesses who are immoral, murderous, and drunk with greed. If you talk with people, you will hear of religions that require effort, works, money and other sacrifices to attain answered prayer, mercy, or eternal life. Or you may hear faith used as a genie of sorts, that if you have enough of it, you can get whatever you want.

On either side there is indulgence and self-absorbed greed. For some religions, it is the gods who are greedy. For others, it is the people.

All those people praying and giving and sacrificing did so because they needed something from God. Those of us who live with illness understand the desperation that can drive a person to tie prayers to a tree or bang a gong or give more, anything to try to get the problem fixed.

Yet the need goes much deeper than whatever current circumstances compel us to try to bargain with, bribe, or appease whoever or whatever has the power to give us what we ask for. The need is a desperation for God Himself. This need will not be fulfilled by anything less than God. We would not be content if the immediate was answered, if we were suddenly healthy or rich or free from pain. We would feel a happiness for a time, until some new form of suffering or loss came, at which time we would start the process of trying to get divine attention again.

No, our need goes beyond the current, beyond the physical, beyond this life. We need a truth to live on, one to base ourselves and our thoughts and actions on. This need causes some to create their own set of beliefs that cater to their personalities and goals. Others follow the beliefs of someone they respect or fear, conforming themselves to it.

No matter what you believe, however, there is truth and there is untruth. You can have immense faith in a medication, but if it is the wrong medication for your illness, it will not help you and could instead harm or even destroy your body. Faith itself is useless and even destructive if it is put into what is not true.

May I please present to you the truth? I am so convinced it is true, I have staked my life and all my eternity on it. If I had medicine that would cure you, and I knew you would die without it, how could I not share it with you? You might not believe me, but if I truly loved you, I could not sit back and watch you die just to avoid making you upset with me. I care too much about you to not tell you, especially since what I have to say is good news!

Here is the truth: God is love. He is not immoral or greedy or lustful. He is just and loves righteousness. This fact, the fact that God is good, gives me cause to worship Him forever. He does not toy with my soul or my pain. He is not selfishly playing with us humans or withholding Himself from us.

God created everything. He created you. He knows your name; He knew all about you before you were even born. He knows where you are, what you are doing, and even how many hairs are on your head. (And considering that we lose about one hundred hairs per day, it means He is keeping track of you at every moment, knowing you and what is happening to you even more intimately than you know yourself!)

I know this is so because God is my loving Father. He has taken me in as His own child and is with me always. He helps me through the day, giving me strength for my weakness and hope when I despair. He gives light for the darkness, and peace in times when peace is impossible. He gives me joy.

I want you to know Him, too. I learned about this God from His Holy Word, the Bible. I know what God is like because He sent His Chosen One, the Messiah, into this world to pay the cost for my sin and yours. He lived and died perfect, and His death and resurrection saved me from a life without purpose and eternity without God. This Messiah is Jesus, and He is my Savior. I came to Him a helpless person full of sin and He washed me clean and gave me new life.

Without Jesus, I would not make it. I would not be able to bear up under the weight of living with disease. I would not be able to withstand the burden of life not being the way it should be. With Him, I have joy and love and peace accessible to me at all times. This joy gives me strength. I know this life isn't all there is, and I have so much to look forward to!

Jesus is the way, the truth, and the life. No one comes to God except through Him (John 14:6). There is no other way. If you have read this book with a longing deep in your soul to know the peace of having a heavenly Father who knows you and cares about you, would you seek Him? God promises that if you seek Him you will find Him, if you seek Him with all your heart (Jer. 29:13), and He is not far from any of us (Acts 17:27).

For me, He is in my heart and my soul, and I want you to have that, too. Knowing God changes everything. I don't have to plead or bargain or beg when I have a need (Heb. 4:16). I can walk boldly right into the throne-room of the King of kings! He listens to me and cares for me, and even when He says no to a request, I know it is for good and can trust Him to do what is best.

I cannot imagine enduring chronic illness without Him, and I don't want you to have to. Please, if you do not know God, or if you are not right with God, or if you've always had the idea that God is far away or doesn't care about you, please seek Him. Read His Word, the Bible (you may want to start with the book of Genesis and then John), and find out the truth. It really will set you free.

Appendix B

Jesus, Healing, and Faith

A Walk Through the Book of Matthew

Searching for Answers from Jesus

by One Who has Not Been Healed

I thought this book was finished, but reading through it one more time I realized something important: I had not faced the biggest questions. What about those verses in the Bible that say if you ask you will receive, and whatever you ask in faith you will get? I had sidestepped those big black-and-white statements by Jesus because, quite honestly, I didn't know what to do with them. They confused me and left me feeling like maybe I'm wrong about all of this. So I avoided them.

However, searching for the truth shouldn't mean searching only the places that feel safe. For my own sake, I decided I needed to dig into the Scriptures again and really face those verses, in each context, searching for real answers even if I didn't like what the answers told me.

I decided to go through the book of Matthew, looking into all the passages I could find about healing and faith and see what I could learn about Jesus and what He did and why He did it. What a treasure chest full of riches I found! Once again, God's Word not only held up to my questioning, but it seems to thrive on it. I have never had one time when I braved seeking the whole truth and did not have that truth set me free.

Would you like to take a walk through Matthew with me? You'll probably want your Bible open to the book of Matthew so you can read the whole passages, and I'd recommend reading the whole book with your own questions in mind. I'll go through from the beginning to the end so you can follow along in your Bible, and we'll look at when Jesus healed lots of people, individuals, why, who had faith, and more. I hope this journey will encourage you as it has me.

Let's get started!

MATTHEW

4:23-24   Jesus begins His public speaking ministry and heals everyone present who needs it. There is no mention of the receivers' level of faith or faith at all.

8:2-4   Heals leper who had faith.

8:5-13   Heals a servant due to his master's (a Gentile's) faith.

8:14-15   Heals Peter's mother-in-law. No faith mentioned.

8:16-17   Heals large group, to fulfill prophecy about the Messiah. No mention of receivers' faith.

8:28-34   Heals demon-possessed person. No faith mentioned.

9:2-6   Heals paralytic when He sees the friends' faith. Does this miracle to show that He has the power to forgive sins.

9:18, 23-26 Brings dead girl to life, father's faith.

9:20-22   Woman who touches His garment is healed. Jesus says her faith made her whole.

9:27-29   Heals blind men, "according to" their faith.

9:32   Heals a mute/demon-possessed person. No faith mentioned.

9:35   Heals large group as He travels preaching the kingdom. No mention of receivers' faith.

12:10-13   Heals a man on the Sabbath. No faith mentioned.

12:15-16   Heals the multitudes following Him. No mention of receivers' faith.

14:13-14   Heals the multitudes following Him. No mention of receivers' faith.

14:35-36   Anyone who touches the hem of His garment is healed. **No one** not healed.

15:28   Heals daughter of Canaanite woman. Mentions the mother's great faith.

15:30-31   Heals the crowds. No mention of receivers' faith.

21:15   Heals those who come to the temple for healing.

Conclusions

Healing of crowds:

During His public ministry, Jesus had multiple times where He healed everyone who came to Him or was brought to Him. In every setting where this happened, **no mention is ever made of any person not being healed because they did not have enough faith.** Considering these events happened often when Jesus first arrived at a place and preached the kingdom, it is very possible there were those among them who did not have faith at all. Jesus' miracles were to show He was the promised Messiah and His preaching was backed by God's power.

Healing of individuals:

There are many different ways Jesus healed and many different things He said to those who approached Him for healing. **There is no pattern.** Jesus dealt with individuals individually. **Never once did Jesus tell an individual they could not be healed because they did not have enough faith.**

Whose faith was required?

Again, there is no pattern. Sometimes Jesus told the recipient it was his or her faith that made him or her whole. Other times He healed based on a father's, mother's or even a master's faith. Many times faith is not mentioned at all as a prerequisite for healing, and sometimes the sick person was too unaware (dead, high fever, demon-possessed) to ask or believe themselves.

When Jesus didn't heal:

There are three incidents in Matthew where healing was not done. One was the demon-possessed boy the disciples could not heal. Jesus said that was because of the disciples' lack of faith, not the boy's or his father's, and Jesus healed him after the disciples could not. The other two were areas where the general unbelief/rejection in that area of Jesus as the Messiah kept Him from doing mighty works, implying **it was belief or unbelief, not a measure of the amount of belief, that mattered.**

Why Jesus Healed:

Jesus never said healing was for the purpose of showing a person's faith. His works of healing were to show He was the Messiah who had been prophesied (Matt. 11:5-6), to show that the kingdom of God had come (Matt. 12:28), to show He had the power to forgive sins (Matt. 9:5-6), and in Matt. 11:20-24, He implies that His mighty works were for the purpose of repentance of the unsaved.

Levels of Faith:

Jesus rarely mentioned a person's level of faith. The two times He mentioned great faith, it was referring to Gentiles (the centurion, Matt. 8:10, and the Canaanite woman, Matt. 15:21-28). Both of those times He spoke of their great faith to or in front of Israelites. The three times He mentions little faith are all to His disciples (when they feared, Matt. 8:26, when Peter sank, Matt. 14:31, and when they didn't understand about the bread, Matt. 16:8).

The Bible
Vs. Health & Wealth

Another walk through the book of Matthew

A Study to Discover God's Perspective

on Health and Wealth

Matthew 4:1-11

Before His ministry began, Jesus denied His own wants and physical needs forty days and then was tempted by the devil to take what He wanted/needed/would rightfully receive in His own way rather than God's. The temptations were to turn stones to bread (get what you need, don't deny yourself), jump from a high pinnacle so the world would see that God will protect (claim the promise in Scripture, show everyone your spiritual status, prove yourself in an obvious way), and take power over the world by worshipping Satan (go ahead of God's timing and God's will and gain success the easier, faster way).

Matt. 6:31-33

If we are not to worry about food or clothes because God knows what we need, and instead are to seek God's kingdom and God's righteousness first, how does that translate to us regarding our health?

Matt. 7:7-11

Though the verses seem to suggest we will get what we ask for, the verses do not actually say we will get what we want, but rather that our loving Father will give us "good things." The passage speaks of a father giving food to a son, rather than tormenting his hunger by something inedible (stone) or dangerous (snake). However, we all know sometimes children ask for things that are not healthy, and a good parent gives good food, which is not always what the child wants. So God knows best what we need, and He will give what is best for us.

Matt. 7:24-27

How do these verses apply to people who think a life of ease is God's will? If the rain, flood and winds are often sickness, discouragement and people judging, what does this passage teach us?

Matt. 7:16-20

Some may look for the "fruit" of our faith in whether we are healthy or not. However, the Bible says the fruits are love, joy, peace, patience, kindness, goodness, faithfulness, gentleness and self-control (Gal. 5:22-23). Are those the fruits we exhibit? Not one of them is dependent on health.

Matt. 7:22-23

Being able to do miracles does not always represent belief.

Matt. 8:2-3

He worshipped and said, "If thou wilt..." Do we forget to worship God and often just come with our needs and wants? Are our prayers mostly about ourselves and how we feel?

Matt. 15:2-11

Religious people brought rules and visible issues to Jesus and He often turned from the issues and went to the heart. If the issue of healing or not being healed was brought to Jesus, what matter of the heart do you think Jesus might address instead? Do you think this issue is similar to those—that people can argue back and forth about who is spiritual and who is not, but in the end only God can see the heart?

Matt. 16:4, 12:38-39

Jesus did not have positive things to say for those seeking a sign.

Matt. 16:24-25

Personal comfort should not be our priority in this life.

Matt. 18:19-20

Was Jesus speaking only to His disciples or to all believers? These verses would imply that if any two believers ask anything, it will be done. This passage is a mystery, but it is interesting to note that it is set right between two passages regarding forgiveness and conflict resolution. It is also of note that verse 19 starts with, "Again I say to you," meaning it is reiterating the previous verse, which is referring to putting an unrepentant sinner out of the church. No verse in this passage's context is about healing or health.

Matt. 20:20-28

People demanding things of God is like the woman asking that her sons be chosen to sit in places of honor in God's kingdom.

Matt. 21: 21-22

This passage clearly states if we pray believing, we shall receive. Jesus was talking specifically to His disciples at the time, when they marveled at a miracle He did. Does it apply to us? I believe that if we are praying according to God's will, yes. If we are praying according to our selfish desires, the Bible says, "You do not have because you do not ask. You ask and do not receive, because you ask amiss, that you may spend it on your pleasures" (James 4:2-3). It is clear God does not want us praying selfishly, using this passage to demand God give us what we want just because we believe.

Matt. 24:24

Signs are not always a show of faith.

Jesus' words against being comfortable in this life:

Matt. 5:11 Blessed are the persecuted.

Matt. 6:19-21 Lay not up treasures on earth, but treasure in heaven. For where your treasure is, there will your heart be also.

Matt. 10:38-39 Take up your cross.

Matt. 11:11 John was the greatest man alive, but still was imprisoned and killed.

Matt. 16:24-26 Take up the cross.

Matt. 19:21-23 If you would be perfect, sell what you have, give to the poor, and follow Him.

Matt. 19:23-24 It is hard for a rich man to get into heaven.

Matt. 24:24 False Christs will show signs and wonders.

Matt. 26:39, 42 Not my will, but God's.

Also in the *Sick & Tired* Series:

The tone is light, casual and non-intimidating.
I feel like I'm sitting cross-legged on the floor
with her talking one-on-one.
...a truly valuable resource
I highly recommend.
- Amy Bovaird
Author of *Mobility Matters*

SICK & TIRED

Empathy, Encouragement, And Practical Help
For Those Suffering With Chronic Illness

Kimberly Rae

SICK & TIRED SERIES SPECIAL ADDITION

LAUGHTER

FOR THE SICK & TIRED

For The Days You Are Close To Crying and Wish
You Had Something To Laugh About Instead!

Kimberly Rae

Her books lift us up
while our wacko symptoms
are trying to defeat us.
- **Marie Miller**
HopeKeepers Indy
39 years of MS

HELP FOR THE
SICK & TIRED

Advice, Encouragement and Humor
From Those Who Understand

Kimberly Rae

...an amazing read
for both my husband and myself
and helped us to focus on us
and not just my illness.
- Jennifer
Chronic Illness Sufferer

YOU'RE SICK
THEY'RE NOT

Relationship Help for People with Chronic
Illness And Those Who Love Them

Kimberly Rae

Excerpt from
You're Sick, They're Not

CHRONIC ILLNESS AND YOUR PERSONALITY TYPE

Health nuts are going to feel stupid someday,
lying in hospitals dying of nothing.
Redd Roxx[xxii]

How did you react when you found out you were officially unhealthy? Not unhealthy as in temporarily sick, but as in chronically I'll-never-be-the-same, what-happened-to-my-life kind of unhealthy?

People react to crisis in different ways. Some jump into fix-it mode and immediately organize and start battling the problem. Others leave the scene and go do something random that has nothing to do with the crisis at hand. Some eat. Others cry. Some rage. Others shop. Some sit and stare at the TV. Others analyze.

And of course, since no one is officially in charge during the majority of crisis events, most of us end up getting frustrated at the way others are acting, or even the way we ourselves are acting.

Why do some of us start emotionally eating while our friends are attacking the problem? Why do some seem to ignore the problem altogether while their spouses are going on about the negative details so thoroughly it makes everyone else depressed?

Are we all slightly insane? Obsessive compulsive? Trying to make everyone around us miserable?

Well, I can't speak for your particular family and friends on those questions, but in general, no, we aren't acting the way we do because of some unnatural, subconsciously vindictive reason. On the contrary, most of us are just acting naturally according to the personalities God gave us.

Wow, you just went from being slightly insane to normal in three sentences. That's got to make you feel good.

Each person is unique, as individual as a snowflake, only much more complex (and we don't melt—way superior). Nevertheless, all our amazing complexities as humans have been narrowed down to four main personality types by someone much smarter than myself. Those types are titled Sanguine, Choleric, Melancholy, and Phlegmatic.

People have different mixtures of these four types, but any given person usually has one or two that are dominant, and tends to follow a certain pattern of thought and behavior based on those dominant types.

See if you can find yourself. And by the way, every type has its strengths and weaknesses, so no deciding your type is great and everybody else's is bad!

Sanguines—like to have fun. Sanguines are bubbly and fun-loving. They like to be the center of attention and tell stories, but tend to exaggerate and be disorganized.

Cholerics—like to have control. Cholerics are the ones who take charge, make quick decisions and like for things to be done the way they think is best. They make good leaders, but tend to be bossy and put tasks over people.

Melancholies—like to have things done right. Melancholies are smart, serious and sensitive. Most creative geniuses are melancholies with their attention to detail and deep creativity, but they lean toward perfectionism and depression.

Phlegmatics—like the easy way. Phlegmatics are easy-going, dry-humor, calm types. They love objectively solving problems and keeping peace, but have a hard time making decisions and have trouble being motivated.

Did you find yourself in one or two of those types? (If you want to study the personality types more in depth, the information in this chapter came from Florence Littauer's book, *Personalities in Power*, used with permission.) I can't tell you how much it helped me and my marriage to realize that my husband and I didn't have to figure out whose reactions were right and whose were wrong. We were both acting according to the personalities we were given by God.

That's not to say we're excused to just act in whatever way comes naturally to us. Like I said, each type has its strengths and weaknesses, and each needs the tempering of the Holy Spirit to be balanced.

That being said, though, it was such a relief to find out that these strong emotional feelings I have in response to my health condition are totally normal for my personality type. I wasn't falling off the deep end or losing my mind, and you aren't either!

Let's go more in depth on each of those four types, including how they tend to react to stress.

A **Sanguine's** emotional needs are . . .

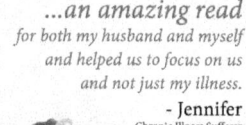

YOU'RE SICK
THEY'RE NOT

Relationship Help for People with Chronic
Illness And Those Who Love Them

Kimberly Rae

Read more in *You're Sick, They're Not!*

Available on Amazon in paperback and ebook.

Lean not on your own understanding.
In all your ways acknowledge Him,
and He shall direct your paths.
Do not be wise in your own eyes.
Proverbs 3:5-7

Available in paperback and e-book.

ACKNOWLEDGMENTS

Any completed book bears the touch of many people who inspired, critiqued, or helped, some even without knowing they did so.

My first thanks goes to Joni Earekson Tada, who I have never met in person, but whose perspective has inspired me since childhood. When I am tempted to feel sorry for myself, living with disease and limitations, I think of her, over forty years in her wheelchair, living for Jesus and others and choosing joy after her own time when life felt meaningless. Thank you, Joni, for accepting a leadership role you never would have chosen, and in doing so strengthening those of us who follow.

Another thanks is due to Brenda Poinsett, another woman I have never met, but whose insights on depression and dark-enabling thought patterns helped me change my ways of thinking. Her book, *Why Do I Feel This Way?*, let me know my experience was not solitary and there were things I could do to fight it, most notably deciding that I wanted to be better. Wherever you are, Brenda, I thank you.

Many thanks to Pastor Robert Setzer, Audrey Setzer, and Bethany Hayes, for being willing to read this book when it was still a manuscript, and passing on your valuable Biblical insights. Your wisdom shared is much appreciated.

It goes without saying that I am thankful to Jesus, for without Him this book would be without hope. I thank Him, and pray He uses this small book, like five loaves and two fish, to feed many who are hungry.

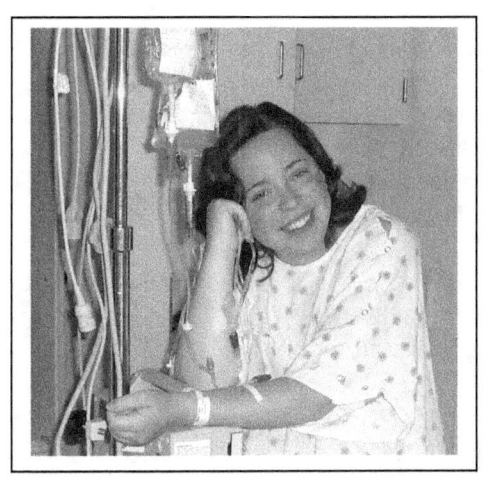

ABOUT THE AUTHOR

Kimberly Rae lived in Bangladesh, Uganda, Kosovo and Indonesia before Addison's disease brought her permanently back to the US. Now a brain surgery survivor, Rae has authored over 35 books and has work in 5 languages. Her Christian suspense/romance novels on international human trafficking (*Stolen Woman, Stolen Child,* and *Stolen Future*) are all Amazon bestsellers.

Rae lives in Madison, Georgia with her husband and two children.

Find out more or contact the author at
www.kimberlyrae.com.

Bibliography

[i] Pack up your Gloomies in a great big box, then sit on the lid and laugh by Barbara Johnson, Thomas Nelson 1993

[ii] Gold by Moonlight by Amy Carmichael, CLC Publications, Reprint edition, 1992

[iii] Lessons I Learned in the Dark: Steps to Walking by Faith, Not by Sight by Jennifer Rothschild, Multnomah Books 2002

[iv] http://quotationsbook.com/quote/10007/

[v] Doing And Suffering: Memorials Of Elizabeth And Frances, Daughters Of E. Bickersteth by Charlotte Bickersteth, Kessinger Publishing, LLC (1860) 2010

[vi] Doing And Suffering: Memorials Of Elizabeth And Frances, Daughters Of E. Bickersteth by Charlotte Bickersteth, Kessinger Publishing, LLC (1860) 2010

[vii] Lessons I Learned in the Dark: Steps to Walking by Faith, Not by Sight by Jennifer Rothschild, Multnomah Books 2002

[viii] *Isaiah 43:1b-2a*

[ix] A Chance to Die: The Life and Legacy of Amy Charmichael by Elisabeth Elliot, Revell 2005

[x] *Keep a Quiet Heart by Elisabeth Elliot, Revell 2004*

[xi] How the Body Works, by Dr. Peter Abrahams, Amber Books LTD., 2007

[xii] http://www.scrapbook.com/quotes/doc/30597/356.html